last
copy

D1711384

MEG
WHITMAN
President and CEO of eBay

FERGUSON
CAREER BIOGRAPHIES

MEG
WHITMAN
President and CEO of eBay

Leslie Alan Horvitz

Ferguson
An imprint of ☑️ Facts On File

Meg Whitman: President and CEO of eBay

Ferguson
An imprint of Facts On File, Inc.
132 West 31st Street
New York NY 10001

Library of Congress Cataloging-in-Publication Data

Horvitz, Leslie Alan.
  Meg Whitman : president and CEO of eBay / Leslie Alan Horvitz.
    p. cm.
  Includes index.
  ISBN 0-8160-5891-1 (hc : alk. paper)
  1. Whitman, Meg—Juvenile literature. 2. Executives—United States—Biography—Juvenile literature. 3. eBay (Firm)—Juvenile literature. 4. Internet auctions—Juvenile literature. I. Title.
  HC102.5.W48H67 2006
  381′.177′092—dc22   2005008906

Ferguson books are available at special discounts when purchased in bulk quantities for businesses, associations, institutions, or sales promotions. Please call our Special Sales Department in New York at (212) 967-8800 or (800) 322-8755.

You can find Ferguson on the World Wide Web at http://www.fergpubco.com

Text design by David Strelecky

Pages 89–108 adapted from Ferguson's *Encyclopedia of Careers and Vocational Guidance, Thirteenth Edition*

Printed in the United States of America

MP Hermitage 10 9 8 7 6 5 4 3 2 1

This book is printed on acid-free paper.

CONTENTS

1

THE EVOLUTION OF A CEO

Fortune magazine ranked her the second most powerful woman in business—ahead of Oprah Winfrey. *Worth* magazine ranked her number one on its 2002 list of best CEOs. *Business Week* magazine named her among the 25 most powerful business managers since 2000. In 2003 she became the recipient of the first annual CBS MarketWatch CEO of the Year Award. *Time* magazine named her one of the most influential people in 2004. But for all these honors and awards, most people have never heard of her— even those who use and cherish the company she runs. Her name is Meg Whitman and she is the chief executive officer (CEO) of eBay, the world's largest online auction company. In presenting Meg with her CBS award, editor in chief David Callaway noted, "At a time when corporate corruption and executive greed is making headlines on a daily basis, CBS MarketWatch wanted to recognize leaders who have excelled in building value for customers, employees, and shareholders."

And no one fits that characterization better than Meg.

Meg did not start eBay—that distinction belongs to a former software engineer named Pierre Omidyar. But since taking over in 1998, when eBay was considered little more than an online flea market (albeit a very successful one), she has transformed the company into the powerhouse that it is today. The statistics are nothing short of staggering: by mid-2004 eBay had more than 105 million registered customers in the United States and some 30 countries, making the eBay community the equivalent to the 11th most populous nation in the world, just ahead of Mexico. Its customers do more than $32 billion of business a year. In 2003 eBay's revenues from listing fees and commissions surpassed $2 billion, with profits exceeding $400 million. Although Meg predicted that eBay would take in revenues of $3 billion by 2005, the company had already exceeded that amount by 2004. In 2000, when she made the forecast, she might have seemed overly optimistic. Not anymore. And although its share price fluctuates—it was about $85 in the summer of 2004 and about $34 in the spring of 2005—the company's value has at various times exceeded that of McDonald's and Boeing.

Meg Whitman, president and CEO of the online auction company eBay, is one of the most powerful women in business. (Corbis)

Yet for a high-powered CEO who is reportedly worth a billion dollars, Meg is decidedly modest and down-to-earth. A striking blond with big green eyes, she's charming, spirited, and easy to get along with. She dresses casually with a workday wardrobe consisting of Oxford shirts, sweaters, and pleated khaki trousers. She wears little jewelry apart from a diamond engagement ring. She prefers to take commercial airliners rather than chartered jets. But her lack of pretension does not mean that she suffers from shyness. When she walks into a room everyone notices. She's articulate and direct. She gets up at 6:00 in the morning every workday and works out for 30 minutes; then she has breakfast with her husband and two sons, whom she usually drives to school. By 8:30 she's already at her desk at eBay's San Jose, California, headquarters conferring with colleagues.

Unlike so many executives who run Internet and software development companies, Meg did not start out in a garage tinkering with computers or designing rudimentary software programs in her junior year in college. In fact, she had no technical expertise or experience at all when she came to eBay. Rather, although she is the head of an Internet company (part of the technology-based *new economy*), Meg worked her way up through more traditional businesses of the *old economy*. (The so-called old economy is made up of *brick-and-mortar* businesses, or companies whose business takes place in brick-and-mortar buildings, as opposed to Internet companies, where cyberspace is often the marketplace.) But in any business the *bottom line* (a company's profit and loss) counts, and so does building a brand name that inspires customer loyalty, which is Meg's specialty.

Meg presides over the eBay empire from what is really a large cubicle. "I haven't been in a cubicle since 1985 because my other jobs have been at more traditional companies," she has said, "but we wanted to reflect our trading community by having offices that are open and allow for free communication and sharing of ideas. . . . Being accessible is really important in our business where information is so valuable." She compares her corporate environment to being on a PT boat (a small armed warship) "as opposed to a battleship." Her PT boat comes equipped with a standard putty desk with a basic PC. Her office has a few interesting personal touches too: Elvis memorabilia and Pez dispensers.

So just how did this unpretentious, practical woman become one of the most powerful—and respected—CEOs in America?

An Unconventional Upbringing

The youngest of three children, Margaret C. Whitman was born in 1957 to an upper-middle-class family in Long Island, New York. It's likely that Meg's father had something to do with her interest in business. He made a good living as a factor for textile retailers. (Factors lend businesses and manufacturers money on accounts receivable. If a company needs money right away, it can turn to a factor rather than wait for its bills to be paid. The factor takes a percentage for the use of the money.) But her father's influence on his youngest daughter was not simply limited to business achievement. A graduate of Harvard University, he placed a high value on education and made it clear that he expected his children to get good grades. He encouraged his children to strive for a high level of achievement but never at the expense of their ethical values. He stressed that it was possible to get ahead in life without walking over other people.

But it was her mother, Margaret, who arguably exercised greater influence on Meg. A stay-at-home mom is seldom described as "adventurous, outspoken, and a can-do woman." But Mrs. Whitman was different. She had an unconventional streak and was not afraid to show it. She told Meg that she could do whatever she wanted rather than be bound by people's expectations. When Meg was a young girl, most women married and became homemakers. Opportunities for advancement in the corporate world were still limited; women were rarely, if ever, chosen to be a top executive or sit on boards of directors. If Meg's life has shown anything, it is that she took her mother's advice to heart.

In 1973, when Meg graduated high school, her mother's stay-at-home life took a sudden and astonishing turn. Two years previously, President Richard M. Nixon had made the first U.S. diplomatic outreach to the People's Republic of China. The warming of relations between the United States and China, bitter enemies only a few years previously, was welcomed by peoples in both countries. Almost overnight Americans fell in love with all things Chinese. Thousands of people were eager to travel to China and see it for themselves. Among the first nondiplomats to be invited to China was the movie actress Shirley MacLaine. Asked to organize a women's delegation, she assembled as diverse a group of women as possible: a Native American activist, a volunteer who had participated in the United Farm Workers grape boycott, and an African-American woman who had been a voting-rights worker in Mississippi. But, as she wrote in her account of the historic trip *You Can Get There from Here*, MacLaine also wanted to find a "conservative Republican housewife person" to balance out her other choices. However, MacLaine did not know any such woman. So she put out feelers, asking friends for recommendations. Someone suggested Margaret Whitman, Meg's mother.

The meeting of suburban housewife and Hollywood movie star was a memorable one. Mrs. Whitman "swept into my New York apartment as if she were about to ride to the hounds," MacLaine wrote. Meg's mother was not the least bit intimidated by the star. "My name is Whitman, and I'm just what you're looking for," she declared, adding, "I'm conservative, tweedy, self-sufficient, and way over thirty." Although she had done little traveling in her life, Mrs. Whitman did not hesitate to join MacLaine's group. China turned out to be an eye-opener for her. Afterward she wrote to MacLaine to say that she was "newly liberated." In fact, the experience proved so exhilarating that she could not wait to return to China. She would go on to lead more than 70 government delegations and tour groups to Asia on her own. Mrs. Whitman's outgoing nature and global perspective were important influences on Meg's own outlook and career.

Showing a Competitive Streak

From an early age Meg demonstrated a strong desire to get ahead. She was driven to excel in whatever she undertook. And she was not content just to concentrate on her studies. She loved swimming so much that she was just five years old when she entered her first swimming competition. She swam competitively through her teens, even capturing state championships; what made her accomplishment even more astonishing was that girls only made up about 30 percent of the school swim teams. "Swimming is one of those sports where how well you do correlates directly on how hard you work at practice," Meg has said. "It also taught me how to be efficient and how to manage time." These were lessons that she would apply to her business career years later.

Managing time was essential, too, if she wanted to do well at school. She managed to squeeze in her homework in the car while she was being taken to and from swim practice or during study breaks. In spite of her crowded schedule she consistently brought home As. In fact, it almost seems as if Meg was in a rush to cram as much as she could in as short a time as possible. It took her only three years to get through high school and achieve such excellent grades that she had no trouble being accepted at Princeton University, which she began in the fall of 1974.

Princeton, however, turned out to be more challenging than she had imagined. With typical ambition she plunged right into her studies, undaunted by the difficulty of the subjects she chose. Although she had decided on a career as a doctor, when she entered Princeton she was disappointed to find that the courses she had selected had little or no relationship to medicine. It was tough. "I survived," she said. "But I didn't enjoy it. Of course, chemistry, calculus, and physics have nothing to do with being a doctor, but if you're 17 years old, you think, This is what being a doctor is going to be about." Then in her sophomore year she took a course in organic chemistry, a notoriously hard subject to master. As Meg said, "That was the end of that." She had all the evidence she needed that she was not cut out for a career in medicine. She began searching for another direction.

Meg discovered what she was good at—and what she enjoyed doing—almost by chance. Between her sophomore and junior years she was offered a summer job selling advertising for *Business Today*, an undergraduate magazine. "It was more fun than physics," Meg said. She had always had an interest in business and regularly read the *Wall Street Journal*, which was delivered to her dorm room. By the spring of her junior year she had abandoned the idea of becoming a doctor and decided to pursue a career in business instead. In 1977 she graduated from Princeton with a degree in economics. "The university inspired me to think in ways that have guided me throughout my life," she told a reporter for the magazine *Fast Times*. (Several years later—in 2002—she expressed her gratitude to Princeton in a very substantial way by donating $30 million to the university intended for the construction of a residential college for undergrads. It was the largest gift by an alumna of the university.)

The following fall Meg entered Harvard Business School. She was only 21 and younger than the vast majority of her classmates. What's more, some of her classmates already had considerable experience under their belt. "I was scared to death," she admitted in an interview with *Fortune* magazine. "On my left was someone who'd been at Chemical Bank for four years, and on my right was someone who'd been in the army for nine years." She found the workload at Harvard Business School to be far more overwhelming than what she had experienced as an undergraduate. She immersed herself in her studies, rarely venturing off campus. "They also tell you 10 percent of the class fails out. For the first year I did almost nothing but work." That might have been the last time that Meg was seriously intimidated.

It was not just the possibility of failure that weighed on her mind. Even in the late 1970s business was not widely considered a promising field for an ambitious young woman. Just 20 percent of Meg's class at Harvard Business School were women. And even then half of the female friends she would make at Harvard Business School (or Princeton for that matter) would end up putting aside their career in order to raise a family. Meg was determined to do both.

Learning Branding on the Job

In 1979, armed with a master of business administration (M.B.A.) degree, Meg moved to Cincinnati to take a job in the brand marketing department of Procter & Gamble, a large manufacturer of household products, among other things. It was an entry-level job, to be sure, but one that allowed her to learn how to develop and market brands. Procter & Gamble has been called "a school for brands" because of its ability to produce and market products that consumers identify with—and buy. As a school of brands, the company also served as a terrific incubator for talent, including such Internet pioneers as Steve Case, who would go on to found America Online; Steve Ballmer, future CEO of Microsoft; and Scott Cook, future founder of Intuit, all of whom worked at P&G during Meg's two-year tenure. Among all of P&G's products probably none is better known than Ivory Soap. Meg was given the task of turning Ivory Soap into shampoo. She had to figure out how to create a new product from an old, well-established one, and then determine how it should be packaged and marketed. To do that, though, she would have to draw on personnel from several departments with a staggering range of skills. But how was she to assemble teams of scientists, technicians, and packaging and marketing experts when she had no authority over any of them?

Meg realized that leadership could be exercised without having to hold a high-level management position. "I learned early on in my career that you could be just as effective, if not more so . . . talking to people about what you were trying to accomplish and enlisting them in the decision." She learned another important lesson at the branding school: Great brands have two components, which she describes as "features and functionality." In other words, the brand has to have attractive characteristics that make people want to have it, and it also has to have a practical purpose that satisfies some need. "In my Procter & Gamble days, it was whiter whites and fresher breath," Meg said. Those are the features. "[B]ut this enabled people to do something they couldn't do before." But features and function alone do not guarantee a great brand. Consumers also have to form "an emotional attachment" to the product. Ivory Soap, for example, is a product that fulfills both the features and functionality criteria, but no one can dispute that people have formed an emotional attachment to it as well, generation after generation.

Within two years at P&G Meg was promoted to manager of brand marketing. All the same, she was growing restless and was beginning to look for new opportunities, not all of which were career-oriented. In 1980 she married Griffith Harsh IV, a neurosurgeon who was just a few years out of medical school. Marriage also led to her leaving P&G. Soon after they were married Griffith was offered a residency at a San Francisco hospital, which meant moving halfway across the country. Meg had no trouble finding work in her new home, taking a job in the San Francisco office of Bain & Company, a consulting firm.

One of her first projects at Bain & Company was to help improve the performance of a division of Saga Foods, which provided college meal services. Characteristically, she did not sit at a desk and try to figure out a solution. First, she needed get a handle on what the problems were, and the only way to do that was to leave the office and find out how the customers themselves felt. So she traveled to several universities throughout the country and talked to food service directors and students. Not only did her research pay off, but it confirmed in her own mind the importance of communicating directly with customers in order to serve them better.

Moving up the Ladder and across Industries

Procter & Gamble and Bain & Company were only Meg's first steps up the corporate ladder. She would go on to hold several increasingly prestigious jobs in top corporations, but not one of them was with a high-tech company. Although the resume she was compiling was impressive in its own right, it gave no indication that Meg was destined to become the head of an online company.

Meg's next job was at Disney, where she served as senior vice president of marketing in the consumer products division from 1989 to 1992. When she joined Disney, the company was about to expand into book and magazine publishing. It was Meg's task to develop a strategy to integrate its new publishing business into the existing entertainment division. She was also instrumental in the acquisition of *Discover*, a popular science magazine. Since Meg had acquired a reputation as a troubleshooter, Disney asked her to undertake an even tougher assignment. The company was in the process of setting up theme stores in Japan. In the United States a brand name like Disney carried a lot of weight, but that did not necessarily mean Japanese consumers would react the same way. Someone had to ensure that the Disney name worked the same magic in Tokyo as it did in Anaheim, California. That was Meg's challenge. At one point she was flying to Japan every month. It was her first attempt to establish an American brand in a foreign country. It would not be her last.

In 1993 Meg traded in Mickey Mouse for sneakers, taking a job with the Stride Rite Corporation, which was intent on reviving its once-famous Keds brand. And as corporate vice president of strategic planning, Meg was also responsible for the launch of its highly successful Munchkin baby-shoe line.

For all her accomplishments marketing new brands or refurbishing old ones, at that point in her career Meg was still largely unknown outside of a small circle of corporate executives. That began to change in 1995 when she joined Florists' Transworld Delivery (FTD), initially as president and later as CEO. In this case Meg had not been hired to resuscitate a fading brand; rather she was being asked to breathe new life into an ailing company. Although FTD was the world's largest floral products company, it was losing money. To turn FTD around, Meg oversaw its planned conversion from a cooperative, owned by an association of florists, into a privately held company, an effort initially opposed by some of the member florists. Not only was Meg expected to make FTD profitable, but she also had to do it in such a way that the people involved accepted the change. That was where her skills in handling people were essential. "Meg was willing to mix it up with florists all over the world," recalled the FTD executive who had recruited her. "She would shake their hands and kiss their babies."

Throughout her career, Meg has been a powerful brand marketing force at companies such as Procter & Gamble, FTD, and Disney. (Getty Images)

Meg implemented a successful ad campaign that packed an emotional punch, playing on the sentimental association that people have with flowers. She also recognized the importance of the Internet as a marketing tool by creating an Ftd.com website, making certain to include every member florist under the FTD corporate banner. But for all her efforts to keep the florists happy, some still resisted the changes she advocated. There was a lot of infighting—too much for Meg's liking. In 1997 she was ready to make her next move.

Having proven that she could market roses and Munchkins to Americans and Mickey Mouse to the Japanese, Meg was ready for a new challenge: toys. Hired as general manager of the Playskool Division at Hasbro, Meg joined a toy company with 600 employees and $600 million in assets. But things were not going well at the Massachusetts-based company. The Playskool division was losing millions before Meg arrived. To turn the division around she had to reorganize it, redesign its product line, and change its advertising strategy. It was true that Hasbro had two hot toy brands of its own—Playskool and Mr. Potato Head—but without Meg's skillful marketing, even these products might not have enjoyed the success they did.

Meg's time at Hasbro reinforced lessons she had previously mastered in her earlier jobs: "Customers really matter, the financial discipline of the bottom line really matters, having a return-based investment philosophy (matters)—I'm spending a dollar on something so what am I going to get back for that?" And one more goal was uppermost in her mind: "Building a company to last." A company, she believes, must have core values. If a company cannot figure out what those values are, then chances are that it does not have them. In addition, Meg believes a company needs good management. As far as she was concerned, it did not matter whether a company was part of the old brick-and-mortar economy or the new wired (Internet-and-technology based) economy: The same economic fundamentals applied in either case. But in 1997, still hard at work at Playskool, Meg had given little thought to joining the new economy. She was doing just fine in the old one. Moreover, she was the mother of two boys, ages 10 and 13, and her husband was happy in his medical practice at Massachusetts General. So when out of the blue a job recruiter called and asked her if she would have any interest in running a small Internet auction company, she did not have to think twice. Her answer was no.

2

INTRODUCTION TO AN ONLINE FLEA MARKET

Often called the world's online marketplace, eBay actually began as a hobby of a software engineer named Pierre Omidyar. There was nothing about Omidyar's career before eBay that would lead anyone to suspect that he would revolutionize Internet commerce. After graduating from Tufts University in 1988 with a bachelor of science degree, Omidyar found work as a developer for Claris, a subsidiary of Apple Computer, where he specialized in consumer applications. He went on to cofound Ink Development Corp., which was renamed eShop and later acquired by Microsoft. He had moved on to a job in program-developer relations for General Magic, a communications software company, when he had an idea for a new website. Omidyar's brilliant idea was to take an old method of buying and selling—the auction—and put it online. If the auction site, which would eventually be named eBay, were to have any chance of success, of course, it would have to be simple and easy for people to understand and use. But what made his idea of an online auction market so remarkable was that it brought people together—usually complete strangers—to buy and sell goods on a person-to-person basis. It would be up to the customers, not eBay, to determine the value of each item. In effect, eBay would provide people with a convenient way of connecting with one another, and then step aside and let them go about their business. By becoming a vehicle for people-to-people transactions, eBay also acquired something that all companies hope for but only a few achieve: passionate brand-name customer loyalty. Thus, eBay would make its money by collecting a fee on the transactions as they occur.

Omidyar conceived of eBay not in terms of a traditional brick-and-mortar auction house, but rather as a "complex adaptive system"—like the stock market—in that it functions on the basis of hundreds of thousands of individual decisions that cannot be predicted in advance. That means that eBay's growth depends on its customers finding one another: Buyers inevitably seek out sellers and vice versa. The result is a company that seems to grow almost organically, as if it were a natural phenomenon instead of a corporation guided by a hierarchy of directors, managers, and consultants.

The Birth of eBay

In 1995 eBay began life as Auction Web with about 20 employees. According to some disputed rumors, Omidyar founded the company primarily as a way for his then girlfriend to sell Pez dispensers. At its outset, however, it was true that a large percent-

Pierre Omidyar, founder of eBay (Landov)

age of the products bought and sold on the site were collectibles of one kind or another.

Omidyar could not have been luckier in his timing. He had gotten in on the ground floor of Internet business. Within a couple of years the Internet would transform the world, just as the telephone and television had earlier in the century. Few companies would reap the benefits from the revolutionary new medium as much as eBay. From the start the new online auction site proved immensely popular. "A monkey could drive this train,"

Maynard Webb, eBay's chief operating officer and technology guru, once joked. "Most of us say, 'Man, we've got something special. Don't screw it up.'"

However, the reality was a little more complicated than Webb's words suggested. Many companies have enjoyed early and unexpected success, only to falter because of competition, a downturn in the economy, or an inability to anticipate changing trends in the marketplace. Because the online auction business was so new and growing so rapidly, no one could predict how eBay would be able to adapt or whether another online enterprise—an Internet behemoth like Amazon.com or Yahoo!—might decide to enter the same business (in fact, they tried) and run eBay out of town. "People were worried that auctions were becoming the Wild West," said Rodrigo Sales, chief executive of AuctionWatch.com, which provides software tools to eBay sellers. On the one hand, Sales observed, eBay (still called Auction Web) was establishing a reputation as "a free venue," where buyers and sellers were pretty much left to do business on their own. However, the company was also under pressure to "to rein in the excesses" so that customers could be assured that they would not be cheated.

It dawned on Omidyar that he was not the person to run the company he had created. If it took inspiration to create a successful Internet start-up, it took wisdom and perhaps even courage to recognize that if eBay were to become a great company it would require skills and know-how that he lacked. So two and a half years after founding eBay, Omidyar decided to find someone else to run it. (Today, Omidyar is a full-time philanthropist investing in institutions and nonprofits that specialize in community development and building support for stronger societies.)

With so many Internet start-ups sprouting in the mid-1990s, there was no shortage of talented managers and entrepreneurs available with some experience in online and software ventures. But when it came to recruiting a CEO for eBay, Omidyar preferred to hire a person who had had extensive experience toiling in the old economy, somebody who kept a sharp eye out for the bottom line.

Searching for a CEO

In 1997 Omidyar approached Ramsey Beirne Associates, a headhunting firm with a wide range of old economy connections. He also enlisted the help of Bob Kagle, a partner at Benchmark Capital, a venture capital company. Like many such firms at the time, Benchmark provided fledgling Silicon Valley software and Internet companies with "seed" money to help them get off the ground; if the company flourished, then Benchmark would turn a tidy profit from their investment. (If the company went belly-up, of course, Benchmark would only have a loss to show for its trouble.)

Beirne came up with the names of almost 40 candidates, among them the CEO of Marvel Comics; the CEO of Sotheby's, the famous auction house; a vice president of marketing at Sears; and the CEO of Hasbro, Meg Whitman. Benchmark's Bob Kagle was particularly intrigued by Whitman. He did not know her personally but he had heard a lot of good things about her. She could build a brand, he had been told, and was capable of "big picture strategic thinking." That was exactly what Kagle felt was needed. Then Beirne broke the news that she had turned him down. Kagle was undaunted. "Go after her," he urged. So that was exactly what Beirne did.

Meg had good reasons—both professional and personal—for declining to take on a new job. For one thing, she had been working with Hasbro for only a little more than a year and enjoyed the toy business. For another, she could not imagine why she should consider giving up a job that put her in charge of a major division at a company with assets of $600 million and several hundred employees, and trade it for the role of a CEO at a small Internet company she had never heard of. Moreover, she saw no reason why she should uproot her whole family and move them across the country. Griffith, who was directing the brain-tumor program at Mass General Hospital, had no wish to leave his job, either. "We aren't going to move our family for this no-name Internet company," was how she put it to the headhunter when he called the first time. But three weeks later she received a second call from the Beirne firm; this time another executive was on the line. "You are perfect for Auction Web, and Auction Web is perfect for you," the headhunter said. "I beg you to get on the plane and come out and meet Pierre and his partner Jeff Skoll, and their venture capitalists."

Reluctantly, Meg agreed to fly to San Jose and meet with Pierre, Jeff, and Bob Kagle, not because she seriously believed that she would take the job, but because she wanted to maintain good relations with Ramsey Beirne's search firm since it might prove useful in the future. The night before her flight she decided to go online and see what she could learn about Auction Web. She could not believe what she found. It looked like an electronic classified-ad section to her and in fact, there was a category called Auction Classifieds. It was "so incredibly boring," she recalls thinking. "I remember sitting at my computer saying, 'I can't believe I'm about to fly across the country to look at a black-and-white auction classified site.'"

But then she reconsidered. Although she was hardly experienced in the Internet business, she was aware of Amazon's extraordinary success selling books. Was it possible that she had overlooked something that Auction Web

At first, Meg declined the job offer at eBay, an online company that many thought of as just a place to sell collectibles such as Pez dispensers. (Associated Press)

offered? So she went back online and spent two more hours exploring the site. It turned out that there was something she had missed. Although Auction Web was a tiny company, it had managed to do $4 million in sales the previous year. But that was not her most astonishing discovery. Auction Web's most remarkable accomplishment was its growth rate: 40 percent a month compounded month after month. An annual growth rate of 40 percent would have been extraordinary. A compounded *monthly* 40 percent growth rate was almost unheard of. Auction Web, she reasoned, must be doing something right.

Taking the Plunge

Meg made a favorable impression from the moment the Auction Web team laid eyes on her. As soon as they began to talk he knew that he had been right to pursue her. "She . . . had a quick wit, a tendency to speak in a burst of single-clause sentences and no shortage of self-confidence," Bob Kagle said. In their first meeting Omidyar spoke about his company as an "enabling" business, one that gave people the power to conduct commerce online that they had never had before. Meg recalled their discussion in an interview with the online magazine Salon. "So I think they wanted marketing skills, the ability to make the right strategic decisions, and the ability to build the infrastructure for a company that would last. Then, I think what was important was that I understood the essence of the eBay community—enabling individuals and entrepreneurs to be successful and build their own businesses."

While she was not ready to make a commitment, she did agree to further talks. She returned to San Jose after Thanksgiving and met with the chief financial officer (CFO). The company had just moved into new offices, but it was evident to Meg that there was still a good deal of work to be done: The cubicles had not even been installed yet. They were not the only thing lacking. Meg found out that Auction Web had no inventory; there was nothing to retrieve, nothing to pack, and nothing to ship. It was a happy discovery. That meant that there were no warehousing or mailing costs, which reduced labor costs as well. This translated into good *gross margins* (the profit that could be made on each item sold). It was as if at the beginning of the game the company already had a favorable position "starting out on the 50-yard line." When she flew back home she was even more intrigued than she had been the first time. She has said that she felt as if she had stumbled "on something that had unbelievable potential."

She met Omidyar again a month later, this time with her family. Not all the news was terrific. The company's phenomenal growth rate had fallen off to nothing in December. But she sensed that the sudden dip in business was a temporary setback. She believed that growth was likely to resume even without any marketing to bolster business. The company was so unique that if she walked away now she knew that she would probably never encounter anything like eBay again. "I think I saw two things," she said. "One was that eBay took unique advantage of the Internet." Essentially, the company had created a business that could not have existed without a medium that could connect the whole world and that operated 24-7. "Then the other thing that I heard from Pierre [Omidyar] was that people had met their best friends on eBay—they had connected over a shared area of interest." That was something that appealed to her; it reinforced what Omidyar had said about how his company empowered people by allowing them to form a community. "I said, 'This is huge.' But I knew that I was coming to a start-up." After all, she was going to have to make a transition from a company with several hundred employees to one that could barely muster 30. She had tackled challenging jobs in the past—but none like this.

She told Omidyar she would call soon with a definite answer. She talked over the move with her husband but in spite of some of the practical difficulties involved, her mind was made up. In February 1998 she signed the contracts. A month later she arrived at the company's offices in San Jose to begin work.

3

BUILDING THE EBAY BRAND

Meg had her work cut out for her. Because eBay was such a new concept, it would take a little while for her to understand how it worked. Her experience in companies like Hasbro and Procter & Gamble could only help her so much in this new environment. After all, it was not as if there was the equivalent of an eBay store in a mall that she could inspect to see how it worked. "You can buy a book on Amazon and it's a great experience," Meg said, "but if all else fails, you can, in fact, go to Barnes & Noble. There's no ability to do what you do on eBay in any other venue."

Getting Down to Business

The creation of eBay could only have been made possible because of the invention of the Internet. So, what lessons from the old economy could the new CEO bring to an

Internet business like eBay? "I have enormous respect for Pierre," she told the business magazine *Fast Company* in 2001. "He taught me about communities on the Web. But what I brought to the table was that I knew what we were going to need if the company continued to grow. My job was to uncover what was going well." That was one of Meg's key strategies. Typically, when new top executives take over a company they are anxious to make their mark. Instinctively, they look for what is wrong and then try to fix it. "That (approach) doesn't actually work very well," Meg says. Looking for problems also offends employees who may feel that their jobs are in jeopardy. "People are very proud of what they've created, and it just feels like you are second-guessing them all the time." Meg prefers to try to find out what is going *right*, which is one of the principal reasons why she has been so successful and commands such loyalty among the people who work for her. As she gradually learned more about eBay, she was sure that she would inevitably come to understand the defects and problems as well. But identifying problems was not her first priority.

Meg set about to build the eBay brand, to make it as much of a commercial magnet for Internet users as Wal-Mart was for bargain hunters in the brick-and-mortar world. But while she was eager to test out her own ideas, she remained in close touch with Pierre Omidyar and Jeff

Skoll so that they could give her guidance as she felt her way in her new role. Her style, as one writer has described it, has always been "collaborative yet decisive, serious but loose," a way of doing business that would serve her well in her new position.

If Omidyar was the visionary, then Meg was the practical hands-on manager. One of her first moves was to put together a marketing plan. Until she arrived on the scene there was not one. It is almost impossible to market a brand before you find out who your customers are. And to do that Meg needed a team of specialists who could collect the relevant data about customers and make sense of them. It was Meg's conviction that the more you knew about your operation and your customers, the more effective the company and the better its bottom line would be. Where Omidyar had hired laidback computer types to run the company, Meg was looking for managers with business experience. She began a drive to bring in management consultants such as Jeff Jordan from Boston Consulting Group and Matt Bannick and Gary Briggs from McKinsey, a well-known consulting firm. Then she installed a new technology team, whom she gave free rein to retool eBay. Her goal was to develop a corporate work ethic and promote eBay culture, which she describes as "a fun, open, and trusting environment."

But even as she gathered new talent around her, she made certain that the recruits understood that she was not interested in a bunch of yes-men or yes-women. On the contrary, if a problem arose, she insisted that everyone speak his or her mind before she voiced her own opinion. That openness did not, however, mean that she had any hesitation about making a decision, even if it provoked opposition.

Getting Through to Customers

Taking a cue from Omidyar, Meg set out to build on the customer base. Competition loomed on all sides. Given the rapid pace of change in the online world, a company enjoying success one day could not necessarily count on being on the leading edge the next. However, Meg believed that if eBay could put together a base of loyal customers and make them feel that they had a vested interest in the company—that it was "their eBay"—then it could thrive no matter what happened. So her major priority was to get people to the site and encourage them to use it without becoming overly concerned about short-term profitability. Profits, she felt, would come later (as they did). She was not running a sprint, but a marathon. By making eBay "the place to go," Meg would be doing what she had done earlier at Hasbro, FTD, Disney, and elsewhere: build a brand name.

Meg recognized that it was the users who created eBay, which she describes as "a vibrant marketplace that enables people to do something they couldn't do before." Previously, if an individual or small businessman wanted to sell a product he or she would usually look for a buyer close to home. What eBay did was to open up the world; instead of tens or hundreds of potential customers, a seller now had millions. "It's like a reunion of people you've never met," one observer put it. That daily—even hourly—"reunion" provides the basis for the eBay community. Says Meg, "We simply try to make it easy and transparent, lay out a few rules and get the heck out of the way."

Of course, customers also want to be sure they are getting as much bang for their buck as they can. As Meg puts it: "I'm spending a dollar on something so what am I going to get back for that?" It's what she calls "a return-based investment philosophy." In fact, maintaining a good relationship with the community is so important to Meg that she rejected a $30 billion buyout offer by the Internet giant Yahoo in 2000. She rejected the offer only hours before it was to be announced because she felt Yahoo might not give the eBay community the attention and importance it was accustomed to. "We didn't just want to be an auction functionality for Yahoo's shopping channel," Meg said.

The eBay Small-Business Connection

EBay has turned into an unprecedented online medium for small business. As many as 430,000 customers make their living selling full time or part time on eBay. The top sellers sell 500 to 1,000 items daily, which makes eBay, in Meg's words, "one of the best places to start a new business, either in the United States or in any of the countries in which we operate." People have actually succeeded in changing their lives. By using eBay to bring in an income, they have been able to quit their day jobs and work at home.

To understand what makes eBay such an important marketplace for small business, you need to think about how products are sold. Products have a life cycle. For example, at first you might not be able to find a specially designed brand-new widget (a fictional product) you have heard about because it has not reached your local Wal-Mart. A few weeks later, though, the shelves are groaning under the weight of the new widgets. In fact, there are too many widgets—the manufacturer misjudged the demand for them and now the stores are overstocked. Or maybe this particular widget came out in time for Christmas and by February customers have lost interest in it. So the retailer will ship most of them back to the warehouses because there is so little demand for them. Or a widget might become obsolete because a better widget has been introduced. That does not mean that the old widget has lost its value. On the contrary, that widget might have a great deal of value to a small group of people who need it for a particular purpose, but because retailers cannot make enough of a profit from stocking them they have become practically impossible to find. That situation is incredibly frustrating to the customers who cannot get them. So the result is *market inefficiency*: too many or too few widgets are produced, or not enough of the right kind of widgets. That is one kind of market inefficiency. There is another kind, too: *information inefficiency*. Customers do not know what types of widgets are available, or they do not have any way of finding out how much of a selection they actually have. Maybe they hope to find a vintage widget, one that is not being made anymore, but haven't a clue where to look for it. And because they do not know how many widgets are available, or what type of widgets, or where to find the particular widgets they are searching for, they also have no idea how much the widget they desire is worth.

Along comes eBay to solve these problems by enabling buyers and sellers to connect in a way that they cannot do by browsing the aisles of a few retail outlets. On eBay a multitude of widgets is available: old and new, in-season and out-of-season, common and vintage. So eBay provides market efficiency since customers can purchase far more widgets at any given time than they could in the brick-and-mortar world. And it offers information efficiency, because the market sets the price of the widgets on sale: If a lot of customers want it, the price will be higher; if few people do, the price will be lower. This gives a customer a much better idea how much to pay. However, eBay has not changed the fundamental law of supply and demand.

EBay has enabled many small business owners to expand their marketplace considerably. Paul Sarver Jr. and Paul Sarver Sr., shown here in their warehouse, own and operate an eBay business that has become the second largest china-replacement company in the United States. (Associated Press, The Morning Call)

Rather, eBay has made it possible for these laws to work better for more people.

What Do Customers Want?

To find out what customers like about eBay and what they expect from it, Meg monitors eBay's message boards. The message boards are the area on eBay where customers have online conversations about different topics, including how eBay is operating. Meg has established a barometer of customer opinions about eBay's management, from Level 1 to Level 10. Level 1 (silent) implies satisfaction, or at least an absence of complaints; Level 10 (hot) means, as one writer put it, that "the community is ready to kill you." eBay's record is pretty good; on average it receives a rating of 3. When changes are proposed for sites on eBay, customers are invited to respond. And respond they do—by the thousands. Without its customers eBay would not be the influential or successful presence on the Internet that it is. "They catch things we don't," says Maynard Webb, the company's tech guru. "The community actually acts faster than we do."

But Meg has not been content to simply monitor customer reactions. She started a real-life forum at company headquarters in San Jose which she calls Voice of the Customer. Meg began the program in 1999 after a longtime customer protested a new company policy (which involved referring losing bidders to similar auctions). Rather than ignore the complaint, Meg and Omidyar went to the customer's city and spent an hour with him, taking notes. Two days later they changed the policy. On the basis of this experience they decided to make a regular practice of meeting face-to-face with customers to get their views directly. Thus was born Voice of the Customer. "Our user community is the best R&D [research and development] lab in the world," Meg says. Every few months, a dozen regular customers are flown to company headquarters in San Jose to meet with Meg and eBay managers and express their ideas about what's working and what's not. Voice is just one component of an elaborate feedback system that Meg has instituted. "At Hasbro, we used to spend a lot of time trying to pick the next hot toy—the next Cabbage Patch Kid, or the next Pokémon," Meg says. "At eBay, we don't worry about that. Our army of users figures out what's hot before we even know." Managers will discuss ideas and policies under consideration to learn whether or not they will work. In one session, for instance, an eBay executive showed off a new feature called "Mr. Lister," which would permit customers to auction off several items at the same time (a proposal that was warmly received). "In our business, we're as close to the customer as you can get," Meg says. "We put a site change up, and in five minutes we already know we have a winner or we have 10,000 e-mails saying, 'What have you done?'" Whatever customers are thinking they make sure that eBay hears about it; 100,000 messages are posted on message boards every week offering tips about good buys to other customers, pointing out problems, or offering suggestions to managers. Anyone can access these postings and join the community. Meg credits Omidyar with "a stroke of genius" for adding a feedback forum where users can learn about other users based on their trading habits. This way regular users can earn a reputation for the quality of the merchandise that they sell and the promptness with which they pay.

Rallying the eBay Community

If eBay users do not find the information they are seeking by reading the message boards, they can attend eBay University. The university is a daylong seminar sponsored by eBay that has been described as "a cross between a traveling business school, an enthusiast's convention, and a religious revival." At these seminars, held in various locations around the country, eBay officials offer tips to veterans and novices alike about how to navigate the site and sell their products with optimal efficiency.

In another move offline eBay sponsors a convention called eBay Live, which was first held in June 2002 and drew 5,500 customers. "Ebaysians" have even planned

People mill about during the eBay Live 2002 Community Conference. Such conferences define the unique community atmosphere that Meg has helped create on eBay. (Landov)

vacations together or gotten together for charitable work— home repairs for an eBay member in need, for instance. But no one could have suspected just how willing the eBay community would be to band together and lend a hand until September 2001.

Meg was on a business trip in Japan when she heard the news about the terrorist attacks on the World Trade Center and the Pentagon. Her chief operating officer, Brian Swette, was in Florida. So the staff had to do what Meg would have wanted them to do if she were in San Jose. First they got in touch with their employees to make sure they were safe. (They were.) Then they initiated a campaign to hold a charity auction intended to raise $100 million for victims in 100 days, which they called the Auction for America. "By the time I was able to call in from Japan our team was already thinking about and acting on the big issues," Meg said. "I did not have to say anything for the right thing to happen." The initiative demonstrated by the management team was no accident. Meg had chosen and cultivated a management team that could act decisively when necessary. The fund-raising effort was greeted enthusiastically not only by loyal eBay customers, but also by companies like Handspring and Palm, which contributed hundreds of personal digital assistants (PDAs) to auction off. And eBay kicked in $1 million on its own. "We've got widows of veterans who are putting up the flags that they were given at their husbands' funerals because they want to contribute to this," Meg said at the time. "We've got moms who are putting up their children's artwork and we've got people from all across America going to their garages, searching their home for things that they can donate."

Because Meg puts so much emphasis on the community of eBay users and identifies so much with them, she is not like a typical CEO. She's more of a first among equals. She is so popular with the customers that people lined up for her autograph at the first eBay Live. One observer at the event marveled at her ability to talk to CD and stamp vendors and then hold a discussion with the CEO of Kodak without missing a beat. And it certainly does not hurt that Meg buys and sells items on eBay herself, including Beanie Babies, children's books, Pokémon cards, and skiing and fly-fishing equipment. "A lot of executives would be comfortable working with other businesses, but not with a person at home selling baseball cards," noted Scott Cook, founder of software company Intuit and an eBay board member. "Meg has a heartfelt understanding of real people. She's an odd combination of homespun and corporate executive."

4

THE TRANS- FORMATION OF EBAY

Although running eBay is no easy task, in its early years the company was much easier to steer than controlling it eventually became. When Meg first took over at eBay she found that she could rely on her instincts in management decisions. But it was one thing to feel her way when there was only a small number of employees; it was quite another to keep a grip on a company growing so rapidly that it passed directly into adulthood without going through the throes of adolescence, as a *Time* reporter put it.

In 1998 the company was registering 34 million auctions. Two years later there were 265 million. Meg had an idea of how to cope with this type of staggering growth: "If it moves, measure it. . . . If you can't measure it, you can't control it." Meg believed that by collecting data, whether it concerned customer behavior or trends on the site, eBay could keep on top of its game.

Monitoring a Booming Business

Meg established a number of ways to monitor how the company was doing. She wanted to know how many people were visiting the site and how many of those then registered to become users. Breaking it down further, she wanted to know how long each user remained per visit and how long the pages on the site took to load. Those statistics were invaluable because they provided a quantitative method of assessing how well eBay was doing while, at the same time, measuring customer satisfaction.

Meg also was interested in eBay's _take rate_—the ratio of revenues to the value of goods traded on the site (the higher the better). How fast was eBay adding new features to the site compared with its rivals? (Answer: about average.) She wanted to know which days were busiest (Fridays in November are particularly hot) and which days saw a drop-off in sales (Mondays in June). This way she would know when to try to stimulate business—for instance, offering free listings to boost the number of auction items available—and when it made more sense to sit back and watch. "Look at growth," she has said. "Look at how much time people spend on the Net and look at the variety of things that they are doing."

Under Meg, eBay became what one writer referred to as "a fire hose of business data." Only after the relevant data is collected can a company decide where to spend its money, where more employees are needed, and which projects are and are not working.

Nonetheless, Meg was careful to maintain a balance between observing and obsessing. At a certain point it is possible to collect so much data that you can drown in it and become paralyzed. "You have to be careful because you could measure too much," Meg said. And she never lost her focus on its core business: auctions. Expansion was inevitable but it would have to be gradual and never lose sight of what had attracted so many customers to the company in the first place. From the start, she understood what makes the company tick. "What is really interesting about eBay," she said in an interview, "is that we provide the marketplace, but it is the users who build the company. They bring the product to the site, they merchandise the product and they distribute it once sold."

But just what kind of marketplace?

Expanding Categories: Beanie Babies to Antiques

Today eBay is known for selling almost every conceivable product from computers to cars to real estate and comic books. But when Meg joined the company it was a far more modest enterprise, specializing mainly in collectibles: Pez dispensers, Beanie Babies, antiques, and coins. Today, collectibles account for only about 40 percent of the articles sold on eBay. Of all eBay's employees—now numbering more than 5,000 (with 2,400 in customer support and 1,000 in tech)—the most important group consists of category managers, a concept Meg appropriated from her days at Procter & Gamble. But whereas at P&G the brands of soap, detergent, and toothpaste were easily categorized, eBay's category managers had a much more daunting task. They had to deal with some 23 major categories (and 35,000 subcategories) that included collectibles, sports, jewelry and watches, and motors. These managers are practically obsessed about measuring the behavior of eBay customers. They are constantly monitoring trends to see what customers are buying, what items are rising in popularity, and which ones are losing interest. It is the category managers' job to identify (or invent) stand-alone categories, giving them a name and a subcategory on the site. Computers were one of the first products to have a category of their own in 1998. Not surprisingly, consumer electronics remains one of eBay's most important categories. In 2003 computers and related sales represented some 25 percent of eBay's U.S. gross merchandise sales. In fact, according to Tech Online, eBay has become the Internet's most successful purveyor of consumer electronics, putting it ahead of Amazon.com and Buy.com. While it varies from one year to the next, the mix is fairly well balanced between new, used, and refurbished computers. And eBay has succeeded in attracting new buyers for so many of the brands of computer and electronic products—up to 50 percent of customers say they are new to the brands—that several major computer and software companies including IBM, Sun, Dell, Iomega, Acer, and Xerox have moved to establish their own presence on eBay.

EBay is also proving very competitive in books, movies, and music, running right behind Amazon.com, while at the same time it is forging ahead in some unexpected directions—house and gardening, for instance, and fine wine, and seasonal tickets to sports events, for example. What might come as more of a surprise is that the company is one of the top car dealers in the country, although car sales still account for only a small fraction of its overall sales. In 1999 eBay Motors was begun as a category after category managers noticed how many customers were buying and selling cars in the Miscellaneous category. "The best thing that we can do at eBay is look and see what the users are doing and then enable that," Meg says. "We think of ourselves as a marketplace steward in many ways."

EBay also has begun to introduce business services as a separate category with a partner called eLance, which

*Pierre Omidyar and Meg show off some of the many items
available for auction on eBay.* (Getty Images)

allows a user to bid on accounting services or a strategy-consulting project or a website designer.

Given eBay's ever-expanding scope, users would expect to find a number of products for sale that defy categorization. After the end of shooting of its film *The Perfect Storm*, for instance, Warner Bros. used eBay to auction off an old sailboat featured in the movie. It went for $145,000. Possibly the most unusual item ever offered for sale on eBay was a major portion of a town. In late 2002 some 80 acres of Bridgeville, California, were put on the electronic auction block. Included in the parcel was a mile and a half of riverbank, four cabins, nine houses, one cemetery, and one backhoe. "We've seen lots of houses and buildings and we've seen land and we've seen bridges, but not a town," a company spokesperson said at the time the listing was posted. Located about 260 miles north of San Francisco, Bridgeville had seen better days. With jobs scarce, residents hoped for a buyer to bail them out and keep the town from dying. Eventually eBay received more than 100 bids for Bridgeville. It seemed that a rescuer had been found in an anonymous West Coast developer who made the winning bid of $1.78 million. But then . . . nothing. No check ever arrived. The disappointed real estate broker decided to forego eBay and try to sell the town in a more traditional way.

Innovations

Once Meg had familiarized herself with the culture and community of eBay, she was ready to make several innovations. She recruited executives from companies such as PepsiCo to institute eBay's first national advertising strategy. When Meg was bringing FTD online she had the good sense to incorporate the home sites of all the florists that were members of the cooperative. There was no reason why she could not do the same for eBay. So she began to court traditional retailers to come on board and join eBay by establishing their own spaces on the eBay site. Sun Microsystems, for instance, now sells millions of dollars worth of its products annually under the eBay umbrella. And as people became increasingly more comfortable buying online, more retailers decided to accept Meg's invitation.

As always, though, her major focus remained eBay's ever-expanding community of users. She opened a customer service center for the thousands of new users. To boost customer confidence she implemented several initiatives, including an insurance program in cases of fraud, and a policy limiting the ability of users to obtain contact information about other members (to prevent unwanted e-mails and identity theft). She also introduced a buyer-protection program through PayPal, eBay's online payment service, which the company purchased in 2002 for $1.5 billion. Meg felt that PayPal would be an excellent match for eBay because it was so easy to use, especially for small dollar amounts that made up so much of eBay's business. Among other advantages, PayPal takes away most of the buyer risk by automatically debiting the buyer's credit card or bank account. That way a seller would know almost immediately whether the purchaser could actually pay for an item. By speeding up billing, paying, and delivery of merchandise, PayPal was a decided improvement over eBay's own transaction service (which was dumped after PayPal's acquisition) and it helped fulfill Meg's ambition of making eBay as accommodating a shopping environment as Wal-Mart.

EBay Goes Public

In 1998 eBay became a publicly traded company, meaning that investors could buy shares in the company on the stock exchange. The initial public offering (IPO), which is when shares are first made available for trading, attracted

The eBay headquarters in San Jose, California (Associated Press)

so many investors that it made the company worth $2 billion in a single day. It also made Meg a billionaire in her own right. Many of the other eBay executives, including founder Pierre Omidyar, also became very rich, but even mid- and lower-level employees who owned shares of the company made out well.

The excitement over the company's sudden fortunes worried Meg. She wanted to make sure that employees focused on the work without becoming distracted by the changes of the stock price. So she imposed a rule that limited employees to checking on the stock price just twice in the workday—once in the morning and once before going home at night. She was right to be cautious; many other tech companies in Silicon Valley were getting caught up in dreams of boundless wealth. Silicon Valley's enthusiastic young entrepreneurs seemed to have forgotten a basic law of economics: What goes up must eventually come down.

5

CHALLENGES, PROBLEMS, AND MISTAKES

Meg told a reporter for *Fortune* magazine in 2003 that missteps could be seen as "learning experiences." Her attitude has always been to deal with problems and then move on. "Most of the time we've made the right decisions, and when we haven't, we've fixed them," she says. But some learning experiences are more painful than others. By tracking trends and measuring data Meg had been able to anticipate problems so she could make course corrections when necessary. But nothing could have prepared her for the possibility that eBay would crash altogether.

The Outage

Technical problems were nothing new to eBay, but what happened late on June 10, 1999, was no mere technical glitch. Prior to this date, the eBay servers were strained with heavier and heavier traffic and outages began to occur with increasing frequency. Yet, while these outages were irritating, none of them ever lasted long. This time, however, the outage went on hour after hour. No one could explain the cause of the outage, and no one could fix it. For that matter, no one could predict when the problem would be fixed. Undaunted, Meg took charge. She did not let her lack of technical experience stop her. It was not long before she had the jargon down, talking about the site's kernel and busy buffer rates with the authority of a computer expert. She vowed to remain in the office as long as it took to bring eBay back on line. She felt that the company's survival was at stake. Other senior management and tech personnel shared her resolve.

That night a room was set aside for people to take short naps if their energy flagged, but no one used it. With pressure mounting, sleep was out of the question. In the middle of the night, as engineers struggled to figure out what had gone wrong, Meg phoned Sun Microsystems, the manufacturer of the eBay servers. Surely, she thought, they would be able to identify the cause of the power outage. She urged the people at Sun to wake their engineers and get them over to eBay's headquarters as soon as possible. But Friday morning dawned with eBay still dark and the problem still unsolved, Meg called an emergency meeting. Things looked dire. The customer service department was practically under siege. Irate customers were firing off e-mails and filling up message boards of AuctionWatch.com, complaining about eBay's incompetence. Small-business people who relied on the site to make a living were especially incensed. "Just so you all know, there are some people whose only income is that generated by auctions," said one message posted on eBay's board. "My business provides income to two single mothers. I can't afford to pay them if I don't have auctions closing." But the news was not all grim. Many customers were still voicing their support. Meg was determined to do whatever was necessary to keep—or restore—customer loyalty. She instructed her staff to do what was needed to respond to the complaints by e-mailing and calling customers and refunding millions of dollars in fees.

The outage persisted for more than 20 excruciating hours before sleepless engineers managed to restore eBay's site. But it would take nearly a month of 100-hour weeks for Meg before the problems could be diagnosed and resolved. To avoid a repetition of the outage, she added redundancy to eBay as insurance so that if the server crashed a backup system would kick in automatically to keep the site up and running. After all, if the technology failed, the company might as well not exist.

Her biggest fear was whether disgruntled customers would desert eBay. "It's like when you crash a car—there are parts all over the highway. You put them back together and there's a clanking sound. You know how a car will never be the same after an accident? Well, I've been assured that that won't be the case here." As it turned out, after the outage eBay was not just as good as before—it was better. Meg's work at building brand loyalty had paid off. A week after the outage, listings had reached 2.2 million, almost back to what they had been before. They went up from there, reaching 4.1 million three months later. In fact, listings were coming in at an astounding rate of more than 300,000 every day. After the ordeal Meg had been under so much stress that she had announced her intention of staying on as CEO for only another few years. But once she saw how the customers reacted, Meg reconsidered her decision to quit. She decided to remain at the helm of eBay as long as employees, investors, and customers wanted her to stay. After the leadership she had demonstrated during the outage crisis that promised to be a very long time.

Consumers versus Analysts

EBay consultants were delighted by the statistics that kept rolling in. In 2001 eBay registered more than 42 million users, up from 22.5 million just the year before. The company now had local sites in 53 cities across the United States and had staked out affiliated companies in five countries. And it was making money—lots of it—with profits of $92 million in 2001, almost double what it earned the previous year. In the spring of 2001 eBay celebrated its half-billionth auction. According to MediaMetrix, eBay also was becoming one of the most visited sites on the Web, with about 14 million visitors per month.

On the rare occasions when she gets away for any length of time, Meg escapes to her husband's family farm in Sweetwater, Tennessee. Or else she slips away to go fly-fishing five or six times a year, using equipment she bought on eBay. She acquired her enthusiasm for fishing from her older son, who urged her to try it. Fly-fishing had a few lessons to teach her about work, too. "Use the wrong fly or miscast your line while fly-fishing and the fish won't bite," a reporter wrote in an online profile of Meg in 2002. "Make a wrong move as the eBay chief and customers will balk, and loudly."

And, as Meg would discover, customers did balk at some of the changes she was beginning to implement, and they certainly made their voices heard.

Now that eBay had become a public company and its stock was being traded on Wall Street, many customers began to feel that eBay had changed, perhaps even lost its innocence, by becoming too corporate. They felt that before eBay went public, the company had acted like it was in partnership with them; afterward, management had different priorities: "Their only objective used to be improving the marketplace," one critic argued, "but after the IPO their objective was to increase the share price." Meg recognized the problem. "We really lived in la-la land with our community for two wonderful years, and it was the time of my life," she told an interviewer. "But once you go public the pressures are completely different. You've got investors and analysts looking at you, you've got the media looking at you, you've got to worry about shares and stockholders and revenue." So it was a matter of maintaining a balance between the users and the analysts. Financial analysts were important to a company's financial health because their recommendations—whether to buy, sell, or hold onto shares of a particular company—could influence whether a stock rose or fell. When Meg met with the analysts they wanted to know whether revenues would be up for the next quarter. But then she had to answer to the community, which would hardly welcome the prospect of increased prices to satisfy Wall Street. Sometimes in its attempt to juggle these competing interests eBay fumbled.

Under Meg's leadership, eBay has faced problems ranging from power outages to economic recessions. (Associated Press)

Burnt Toast

One example of an eBay fumble was a controversial toaster ad that turned up on the eBay search page in May 2000—but only if the user specifically requested information on toasters. The ad was a modest one as these things go: It had a small picture of a toaster with a piece of bread in it. The ad copy read: "Is your old toaster crummy? Save $15 on appliances and more." Although this may sound innocent enough, the ad linked anyone who clicked on it to OurHouse.com, an online site that sold appliances for

Ace Hardware. To outraged customers, who voiced their indignation on message boards and in hundreds of e-mails, the ad indicated that eBay was interested only in the money it could make by selling ads. It did not seem to matter to eBay that in its pursuit of extra revenues it would take ads from companies that were, in effect, competing with eBay's own customers. In other words, if one customer was lured to a company's site to purchase a toaster, another eBay customer trying to sell a toaster on eBay might lose out on a potential sale. That led to charges by some users that eBay was basically abandoning the thousands of small-business people who used the site and depended on it for their income. "People can't pay their bills, their rent or mortgage," a disgruntled customer declared on AuctionWatch.com's eBay board. "They can't buy books for their kids' school. Their mother gets booted out of the nursing home."

Although eBay was hardly the cruel or ruthless corporation that such a depiction suggests, Meg was quick to realize that the toaster ad had been a big mistake. The customers won the battle. To avoid rankling customers further, eBay has refused advertising from other companies that would have doubled its revenue. But given her dual obligations and loyalties—to Wall Street on the one hand and the community to the other—there was no way that she could entirely satisfy customers who believed that the old neighborly eBay they had grown to love was gone for good.

The Auction House Stumble

The feeling among some customers that eBay was headed in a bad direction was reinforced when the company acquired Butterfield & Butterfield, a San Francisco auction house, in 1999 for $235 million of eBay's stock. Compared to the two prestigious traditional auction houses, Sotheby's and Christies, Butterfield & Butterfield was a minor player. In fact, eBay had previously flirted with the idea of forming an alliance with Sotheby's but eventually backed out because it did not seem to be a proper fit. Nonetheless, eBay was interested in branching out into a more upscale market, selling fine art and rare collectibles. "There are only so many Beanie Babies and old records you can sell," observed one Wall Street analyst. But many customers expressed dismay over the Butterfield decision. They looked on the auction house as a presence that did not really belong on the eBay site, where it was integrated into a category called Great Collections. Even though eBay offered significant protections for customers purchasing items on the Great Collections site—a five-year guarantee of authenticity and a 30-day money-back guarantee that the item was exactly what it was advertised to be—prices were too high for most of eBay's customers. And there was a problem attracting sellers as well. It also turned out that there were some things that a brick-and-mortar high-end auction house like Sotheby's could do that could not be duplicated online. But the larger problem seems again to have come down to a rare misjudgment on eBay's part to go upscale at the risk of alienating eBay's users. In 2002 eBay sold Butterfield & Butterfield for what was called an "immaterial gain."

The Controversial AOL Alliance

A move by eBay to forge an alliance with AOL also provoked protest from a number of customers. Under the arrangement AOL would sponsor ads for its service on eBay. A company spokesperson explained it this way to a *Wall Street Journal* reporter: "The (eBay) management team is recognizing that there is a significant opportunity to monetize the site to a greater degree than we have in the past." (Monetize means simply make more money.) It was "a move to the dark side," complained an indignant customer whose view reflected that of other disenchanted community members. "Members visit eBay to buy, to sell, to shop, to compare, to talk, to grow their communities. Not for advertising. Not for 'messages,' however 'targeted' those messages may be. The fact that eBay's constituency is huge doesn't make that constituency an 'audience.'"

Once again a move that was meant to please Wall Street did not necessarily go over well with eBay users.

Riding Out the Internet Bust

Until the spring of 2001 the high-tech market looked solid to many investors. But for thousands of entrepreneurs and their employees who had nurtured dreams of becoming multimillionaires and retiring by the time they turned 30, a rude awakening was in store. In April 2001 the NASDAQ index, which measured the stock performance of hundreds of high-tech companies, suddenly plunged. The Internet bubble had burst. Ebay couldn't entirely escape the bloodbath. Its stock fell to a low of $30 a share, its worst showing since going public. The setback proved temporary, however. While other Internet-based companies suffered a severe loss of business in the ensuing downturn or went out of business altogether, eBay managed to regain its footing. In fact, the recession offered opportunities that few other Internet-based companies were in a position to exploit.

In an interview with *Fast Company* in the aftermath of the NASDAQ crash, Meg expressed the kind of optimism that had become a rare commodity in Silicon Valley. "Our hypothesis is that in a slowdown, eBay actually benefits," she said. "And that's because buyers still want the things that they want. Consumer electronics, computers, whatever." At the same time, she noted, in a recession people were likely to become "more value-oriented." They did not have as much cash to throw around, so they wanted to be certain they were getting their money's worth. And where better to get good value for your money than on eBay? Meg even went so far as to forecast an increase in business as sellers went on the site to sell goods they did not want or really need in order to raise extra cash.

She was right. There was another reason that eBay flourished while other Internet companies were gasping for air. By 2001 an increasing number of people in the United States and abroad had become used to making purchases online. And more people were comfortable with an auction formula rather than simply buying from companies that offered items at a fixed price.

Responding to Fakery and Fraud

A reporter for the *New York Times* observed that eBay sellers have such "unrivaled power" that buyers "chase the single largest selection of items for sale and accept whatever conditions" eBay imposes. But there is a downside to being the largest and most popular auction site on the Web.

In 2003 online purchasers lost $200 million as a result of online fraud. Half of the 166,000 complaints about fraud made to the Federal Trade Commission involved online auctions—and most of them were conducted on eBay.

In the real world, as Adam Cohen points out in *The Perfect Store*, his portrait of eBay, there is a long, if not exactly honorable, tradition of what is called shill and "phantom" bids in which the seller, using a false identity, pretends to bid for the item with the intent of driving up the price. In the online world this practice is even easier than in the brick-and-mortar world because the seller can hide behind any number of fake identities with little fear of detection. There are other kinds of fraud as well. Many customers have been deceived by phony listings where goods are overvalued or do not exist at all. In one instance, someone pretended to put human organs on sale, which would be illegal in any case. In 2000 there was a lot of interest in a painting by a well-established artist named Richard Diebenkorn that commanded a bid of $135,000, until it was revealed that the work was a fake. Travel voucher fraud also has been a big headache for eBay. The most prevalent problem, though, continues to be fraudulent listings for high-end consumer goods such as plasma televisions, laptop computers, mountain bikes, espresso machines, treadmills, and telescopes. Sellers will sometimes embellish their listings with elaborate descriptions and photos to convince the would-be buyers that the items are genuine. There have been instances where sellers post multiple fake listings at once to swamp a category. To defend its users, eBay has put 800 people on the payroll worldwide whose only job is to protect users against fraud. If eBay suspects that a fraudulent transaction has taken place it sends alerts to the winning bidders, warning them not to complete the transaction. That was how the fake Diebenkorn painting was caught. The company also points out that at any given time only 2,000 items out of an average of 20 million items on sale—or one-hundredth of 1 percent—are fraudulent.

In an attempt to prevent multiple false listings, eBay also has installed special software called Shill Bidder, which detects unusual patterns of bids to identify fraudulent behavior. But critics complain that eBay does not use the software enough to catch much fraud and that the company's software is not up to the task.

Unlike a traditional auction house such as Sotheby's or Christie's, eBay cannot guarantee buyer satisfaction. A traditional auction house is obligated to make certain of a work's origin before it can put it up for sale. Moreover, potential bidders have the chance to inspect the goods they are interested in. None of this is true on eBay, where a customer has to rely on a description of an article.

Whether well founded or not, some customers believe that eBay is not doing enough to fight fraud, so they have decided to take matters into their own hands. They have become what the *New York Times* called "eBay vigilantes." These vigilantes believe that eBay has deliberately hidden the extent of fraud on its site in order to protect its brand. They point out that eBay does not count many types of fraud, such as scams using Western Union. Some vigilantes feel that they have no choice but to become investigators themselves and track down the sources of fraud.

Rob Chesnut, eBay's vice president for rules, trust and safety, told the *Times*, "We love it that people want to help, but there's a right way to do it and a way that isn't constructive or in the interest of a good community marketplace." At the same time he cautioned the vigilantes against taking action on their own since they might act hastily on bad information and try to interfere with legitimate auctions: "Just like in the offline world," he said, "you can't have people running around taking the law into their hands."

"Our best ideas are our customers' ideas," Meg has said. But that does not stop them from also being the source of a lot of bad ideas from time to time.

6

FACING THE FUTURE

"There is no industry in which we compete, really," Meg has said. "There is no online marketplace industry. We are pioneers." No one seriously disputes eBay's pioneering role on the Web (or in the real world for that matter). And no online auction company can compete with eBay in the way that, for example, General Motors competes with Ford Motor Company. But that is not to say that eBay does not have to worry about challenges from other companies. What's more, when Meg took over eBay in 1998 the companies that were ready to pounce had deep pockets and very recognizable brand names of their own, including Amazon.com, Yahoo, and Lycos (the Internet search engine). In addition, Priceline's new car auctions were threatening to edge in on the market staked out by eBay Motors.

Facing the Competition

Under Meg's direction, eBay has proven quick to respond and outmaneuver its potential rivals. When Yahoo attempted to grab a share of the online auction market in 1998, it tried to outflank eBay by dropping fees on sales altogether. In spite of the challenge Meg and her team resisted the idea of eliminating commissions. They soon realized that the commissions actually served an important screening function: While they did not appreciably discourage legitimate sellers, they did deter people from listing junk because it did not cost them anything. The result was that eBay maintained a reputation among its customers for value that Yahoo could not match.

Amazon.com presented a more serious threat. When Amazon, which began as an online bookseller, opened its own auction site in 1999, Meg realized that it would be perceived as a force to be reckoned with. She immediately got on the phone to reassure anxious Wall Street financial analysts, insisting that they had nothing to fear from the new Amazon venture. She told them that eBay had the benefit of experience and an established customer base. Moreover, a close examination of the Amazon site revealed other drawbacks. For example, it offered no chat rooms or discussion boards; in fact, it lacked any way for customers to communicate with one another at all. Nonetheless, some of eBay's own employees remained concerned. Amazon might be new to the auction game but it had proven to be a formidable retailer, selling products ranging from books to CDs and toys. But it turned out that Meg was right to discount Amazon's challenge. Amazon's auction site was mostly used by big businesses—hardly like the typical sellers who made up the majority of eBay's customer base. But Meg also recognized that Amazon had introduced some useful new features that eBay could incorporate, including an innovative password-retrieval system, a listing of items available in a customer's hometown, and notification when a desired item became available. And Amazon had something else that eBay could use: a much more efficient credit card processing capacity.

Sometimes Meg did not even wait for a challenge from a competitor to develop. If Amazon and Yahoo were experimenting with auction sites, she thought, could AOL be far behind? With more than 20 million subscribers, AOL had a ready-made pool of customers to draw from if it opened its own auction site. Rather than wait for that to happen, she worked out a deal with the company, making eBay AOL's exclusive auction provider. This move essentially ensured that eBay would not have to face competition from AOL. By adding AOL's vast customer base to that of eBay, Meg also helped create what is known in business circles as the *network effect*. The network effect is based on building a critical mass: The more buyers available, the more sellers will want to use the site. That in turn leads to more buyers—and more sellers.

Making New Acquisitions

Even as eBay outdistanced its competition, its rapid growth presented Meg with another daunting challenge: By 2003 the site was handling band traffic (Internet activity) that was much larger than it had just three years ago both in terms of page views and gigabytes. (A *page view* refers to a Web page that has been viewed by one visitor. Advertisers are especially sensitive to the number of views a page promoting their product receives.) By this point eBay dominated nearly 80 percent of the online auction market. But how was such astonishing growth to be managed? In the past she had focused on finding out what customers were buying, selling, and shunning. But expansion was not just a matter of adding more subcategories. Meg opted for a strategy that called for expansion in two directions: acquiring new businesses on the one hand, and establishing new outposts in America and overseas on the other. But she had to exercise careful guidance. A company could become too big and bloated, too slow to respond to fast-moving developments in the marketplace.

When Meg looked for potential acquisitions she was interested in finding companies that would complement eBay. To capitalize on China's burgeoning economic growth eBay bought NeoCom Technology, Taiwan's leading operator of auction-style websites, and acquired a large stake in EachNet, an online trading community in China. In Europe she moved to acquire iBazar, a European auction site that was beating eBay in France and Italy, for about $126 million, a bargain given the fact that the original asking price in 2000 was close to $1 billion.

But no potential acquisition was more important than Half.com, the third most-visited website at the time. Unlike eBay, Half.com sold goods at set prices—often as one-day specials—rather than through auctions. Half.com's popularity made it a takeover target, especially for an overseas company eager to hone in on eBay's market. What made Half.com so intriguing to Meg was the way it listed its products. A customer looking for a popular book, for example, would find several copies at different prices and in various conditions. Some might be new, others secondhand. Conversely, customers could sell a book online and set the price they felt it was worth, based on its condition. Once eBay bought and incorporated it into the site, the management team went to work expanding the categories that it offered to woo buyers who preferred fixed prices to bidding for goods.

EBay as a Platform

In addition to making new acquisitions Meg also had to think about eBay's growing number of partners—companies that were building businesses that provided services to support trading on eBay. The relationship between these companies and eBay could be considered symbiotic since without eBay these companies could not function (or in many cases even exist). At the same time, by providing valuable services to customers, they helped eBay. These relationships have made eBay into what is known as a platform. "We're so well-served by letting others think about how to make this platform even more powerful," Meg said. Microsoft, too, is another example of a platform. Many other companies have flourished by providing services for Microsoft users, such as software for the Microsoft Windows operating system. But Meg dismisses the comparison. By making so many other companies dependent on it, Microsoft has become such a dominating force in the marketplace that it threatens to become a monopoly, gobbling up smaller competitors. That is not the kind of platform that Meg believes eBay has become. She points out that eBay is not competing with other companies the way that Microsoft is; it is competing for consumer dollars. And consumers have a lot of other places to turn if they prefer to make their purchases elsewhere—a far cry from a situation in which nearly every PC on sale comes with Windows already installed.

Expanding Abroad

Geographical expansion was a different, and sometimes more complicated, matter. In the United States eBay established local sites in more than 60 cities including New York, San Francisco, and Houston. Worldwide, eBay has expanded to nearly 30 countries from Germany and France to Australia and New Zealand. In its pursuit of global expansion eBay has seriously stumbled only once— in Japan. In 2002 Meg pulled eBay out of the country, the world's second largest economy. The problem was that Yahoo had arrived first and already established such dominance over the online auction market that eBay stood little chance of making inroads. Nonetheless, eBay was reaping ever-increasing revenues from its foreign ventures. In the fourth quarter of 2002 alone, eBay pulled in about $109 million in revenues, up an incredible 173 percent from the same period the year before. But eBay was only getting its feet wet in a global market worth $1.8 trillion, which, as Meg put it, "is a very big sandbox for a company like eBay."

But running a virtual global empire is far from simple; new currency-conversion software had to be installed to allow people to more easily buy goods denominated in

Meg has helped eBay expand its presence across the globe. Pictured here is an employee at the eBay EachNet office in Shanghai, China. (Landov)

currencies other than their own, for instance. And a translation capability was necessary so that customers using different languages could understand one another well enough to buy and sell. And before eBay could do business it also had to conform to all the legal and regulatory requirements of each country without jeopardizing the ability of customers in other countries from buying and selling items as easily as they would if international boundaries did not exist. "It's complicated," Meg admits.

"We are pioneering new ground here. You can go to eBay.fr [the company's French site], but you can also go to eBay.com [the company's U.S. site]. The same is true for eBay.de [Germany]." But she acknowledged that the process was going to take time and that mistakes were inevitable. She said that eBay would have to "navigate the snakes," adding that "sometimes you're going to get a toe bitten off." So far most of her toes seem to be intact. "It's fun, but just keeping the communication and making sure that eBay Germany understands the mission and is executing similarly to eBay Australia or eBay U.K. is a real challenge."

But Meg points out that eBay has had one great advantage: It did not have to be perfect. "This is not diplomatic relations. This is not military secrets. This is trading $50 to $100 items." Pretty good might not be perfect but pretty good would serve the needs and expectations of most of the company's customers. What really seems to excite Meg about eBay's expanding role in the global marketplace is its potential to create an unprecedented type of international trade—not among nations but among individuals, particularly people who have been left behind by globalization. "You think about the third world, villagers in Guatemala and Africa who have handicrafts to sell, who could list in their currency and their language and sell to the industrialized world," Meg said. "EBay is creating new trade on a global basis that the world has never seen—that's what gets us up in the morning." As people sell their products they bring in more money for their towns and villages. That gives them the wherewithal to buy more of what they need and want from the developed countries. Meg believes that an online marketplace that knows no borders can "empower people to make a living in ways they could not before eBay."

Looking Ahead

When asked how she views eBay's future, Meg responds with characteristic modesty. "When is this new way of doing business [on the Web] not perceived to be new anymore? I don't know when that is—in the next five years, maybe, in the U.S. But the Web is new, e-commerce is new, and eBay is newer yet. To have eBay be as accepted as taking a trip to Wal-Mart, I think we may be quite a long way from that." Meg sees herself as a strategist, not merely as a leader of a company. How will eBay grow? What new acquisitions will best fit its business? How can the company continue to build a global enterprise where goods and services are bought across borders every day? It is her job—her mission—to determine what she terms "the long-term road map" that will shape the future for eBay over the next several years.

Even after several years at eBay's helm Meg still loves her job. There are always new challenges, ones that she never anticipated. "When you come into work every day . . . there are decisions that have to be made where they've never been made before[,] because we created this entirely new marketplace." How do you figure out what to do when you do not have much experience to fall back on? New territory is being charted all the time at eBay. Many companies rely on a top-down structure: Management decides to make a product or deliver a certain service, and then the employees have the responsibility of implementing the decision. Then everyone has to wait to see whether the consumers go for it. But that is not the way eBay operates. Consumers have a big say in what eBay will or will not do. "It is incredibly fun to see entrepreneurs take advantage of this marketplace and utilize it in ways that we never would've dreamed," Meg says. It was eBay's users who came up with the idea of selling used cars on eBay—something Meg says she probably would never have thought of on her own. "You know, if you said from Beanie Babies to used cars, I'm not sure I would've gotten there."

Ultimately, it is the eBay customers who matter most to Meg, and to the business of eBay itself. And when asked to describe eBay's main competitor, Meg has said, "It's not the other online auction companies. It's the challenge of

Meg's success at eBay and other companies has largely been the result of her ability to never forget the needs of the customer. (Landov)

getting people to do on eBay what they do in the offline world. . . . So our challenge is actually to get the offline transactions transferred online because it's more efficient, more fun, and there's a bigger selection. Our real competitor is, in many ways, the old way of doing things."

TIME LINE

1957   Born in Long Island, New York, the youngest of
three children

1957–   Grows up and attends elementary and high school
1973   in Cold Spring Harbor, Long Island, New York

1974   Graduates high school in three years and is
accepted at Princeton

1977   Graduates Princeton with a BA in economics

1979   Graduates Harvard Business School with an MBA

1979–   Takes her first job at Procter & Gamble Company in
1981   Cincinnati where she works in brand management

1980   Marries Griffith Harsh IV, a neurosurgeon

1981   Gives birth to her first child—a boy

1982–   Moves with her family to San Francisco to assume a
1989   job as vice president at Bain & Company, a consulting company

1984   Gives birth to her second child—also a boy

1989–   Develops her branding skills as senior vice president
1992   of marketing of the Disney Consumer Products
Division

1992–   As president of the Stride Rite Division launches the
1993   highly successful Munchkin baby shoe line and
revamps the Stride Rite brand and retail stores; also
serves as executive vice president for the Keds
Division and corporate vice president of strategic
planning

1995   EBay started in 1995 under the name Auction Web
by software engineer Pierre Omidyar

1995–   As president and CEO overhauls Florists Transworld
1997   Delivery (FTD), the world's largest floral products
company, overseeing its transition from a florist-
owned association to a for-profit, privately owned
company

1997–   Moves to toy maker Hasbro Inc. as general manager
1998   of the company's Playskool Division, assuming
responsibility for global management and marketing of two of the world's best-known children's
brands: Playskool and Mr. Potato Head

1998   Joins eBay (Auction Web) as president and CEO
after Omidyar relinquishes direct control over the

company he founded; eBay goes public, its shares becoming actively traded on the NASDAQ

1999 EBay experiences several power outages that cause the site to crash, including one that lasts almost 24 hours; eBay acquires San Francisco auction house Butterfield & Butterfield to sell high-end antiques and paintings; Amazon.com launches an auction site but fails to knock out eBay's business

2000 A fake painting purportedly by noted American artist Richard Diebenkorn is nearly sold on eBay for $135,000 before the fraud is uncovered; tech-heavy NASDAQ reaches its peak; the fallout from the collapse of Internet stocks causes many companies to retrench or go out of business, but eBay rides out the bust; a controversial ad for another company's toaster on the eBay site arouses consumer anger and the ad is quickly pulled; by the end of the year eBay is generating $59 million a day or $684 per second; valued at $32 billion, it now has affiliates in 7 countries; Meg rejects a $30 billion buyout offer from rival Yahoo

2001 EBay holds its half-billionth auction; eBay launches its 100-day $100 million campaign to benefit victims of the 9/11 terrorist attacks

2002   *Fortune* magazine ranks Whitman the third most powerful woman in business in 2002; *Worth* magazine ranks her number one on its 2002 list of best CEOs; *Business Week* magazine names her among the 25 most powerful business managers annually since 2000; eBay pulls out of Japan, the world's second largest economy and Internet user, when it became clear that Yahoo! Japan had taken an insurmountable lead; eBay buys PayPal for $1.5 billion to process transactions more quickly; Meg makes a $30 million donation to Princeton intended for the construction of a residential college for undergrads, the largest gift by an alumna of the university

2003   EBay has more than 105 million registered customers in the United States and 30 other countries, making the company equivalent to the 11th most populous nation in the world, just ahead of Mexico; it is now doing more than $32 billion of business a year with revenues from listing fees and commissions surpassing $2 billion; CBS MarketWatch names Meg Whitman its first CEO of the Year, citing her for "her achievements in building the online auctioneer and creating value for both employees and shareholders"

HOW TO BECOME A BUSINESS MANAGER

THE JOB

Management is found in every industry, including food, clothing, banking, education, health care, and business services. All types of businesses have managers to formulate policies and administer the firm's operations. Managers may oversee the operations of an entire company, a geographical territory of a company's operations, or a specific department, such as sales and marketing.

Business managers direct a company's or a department's daily activities within the context of the organization's overall plan. They implement organizational policies and goals. This may involve developing sales or promotional materials, analyzing the department's budgetary requirements, and hiring, training, and supervising staff. Business managers are often responsible for long-range planning for their company or department. This involves setting goals for the organization and developing a workable plan for meeting those goals.

A manager responsible for a single department might work to coordinate his or her department's activities with other departments. A manager responsible for an entire company or organization might work with the managers of various departments or locations to oversee and coordinate the activities of all departments. If the business is privately owned, the owner may be the manager. In a large corporation, however, there will be a management structure above the business manager.

Jeff Bowe is the midwest general manager for Disc Graphics, a large printing company headquartered in New York. Bowe oversees all aspects of the company's Indianapolis plant, which employs about 50 people. When asked what he is responsible for, Bowe answers, "Everything that happens in this facility." Specifically, that includes sales, production, customer service, capital expenditure planning, hiring and training employees, firing or downsizing, and personnel management.

The hierarchy of managers includes top executives, such as the president, who establishes an organization's goals and policies along with others, such as the chief executive officer (CEO), chief financial officer (CFO), chief information officer (CIO), executive vice president, and the board of directors. Top executives plan business objectives and develop policies to coordinate operations between divisions and departments and establish procedures for attaining objectives. Activity reports and financial statements are reviewed to determine progress and revise operations as needed. The president also directs and formulates funding for new and existing programs within the organization. Public relations plays a big part in the lives of executives as they deal with executives and leaders from other countries or organizations, and with customers, employees, and various special interest groups.

The top-level managers for Bowe's company are located in the company's New York headquarters. Bowe is responsible for reporting certain information about the Indianapolis facility to them. He may also have to work collaboratively with them on certain projects or plans. "I have a conversation with people at headquarters about every two to three days," he says. "I get corporate input on very large projects. I would also work closely with them if we had some type of corporate-wide program we were working on—something where I would be the contact person for this facility."

Although the president or chief executive officer retains ultimate authority and responsibility, Bowe is responsible for overseeing the day-to-day operations of the Indianapolis location. A manager in this position is sometimes called a *chief operating officer* (COO). Other duties of a COO may include serving as chairman of committees, such as management, executive, engineering, or sales.

Some companies have an executive vice president, who directs and coordinates the activities of one or more departments, depending on the size of the organization. In very large organizations, the duties of executive vice presidents may be highly specialized. For example, they may oversee the activities of business managers of marketing, sales promotion, purchasing, finance, personnel training, industrial relations, administrative services, data processing, property management, transportation, or legal services. In smaller organizations, an executive vice president might be responsible for a number of these departments. Executive vice presidents also assist the chief executive officer in formulating and administering the organization's policies and developing its long-range goals. Executive vice presidents may serve as members of management committees on special studies.

Companies may also have a *chief financial officer* or *CFO*. In small firms, the CFO is usually responsible for all financial management tasks, such as budgeting, capital expenditure planning, cash flow, and various financial reviews and reports. In larger companies the CFO may oversee financial management departments to help other managers develop financial and economic policy and oversee the implementation of these policies.

Chief information officers, or *CIOs*, are responsible for all aspects of their company's information technology. They use their knowledge of technology and business to determine how information technology can best be used to meet company goals. This may include researching, purchasing, and overseeing the set up and use of technology systems, such as intranet, Internet, and computer networks. These managers sometimes take a role in implementing a company's website.

In companies that have several different locations, managers may be assigned to oversee specific geographic areas. For example, a large retailer with facilities all across the nation is likely to have a number of managers in charge of various territories. There might be a midwest manager, a southwest manager, a southeast manager, a northeast manager, and a northwest manager. These managers are often called *regional* or *area managers.* Some companies break their management territories up into even smaller sections, such as a single state or a part of a state. Managers overseeing these smaller segments are often called *district managers,* and typically report directly to an area or regional manager.

REQUIREMENTS
High School

The educational background of business managers varies as widely as the nature of their diverse responsibilities. Many have a bachelor's degree in liberal arts or business administration. If you are interested in a business managerial career, you should start preparing in high school by taking college preparatory classes. According to Jeff Bowe, your best bet academically is to get a well-rounded education. Because communication is important, take as many English classes as possible. Speech classes are another way to improve your communication skills. Courses in mathematics, business, and computer science are also excellent choices to help you prepare for this career. Finally, Bowe recommends taking a foreign language. "Today speaking a foreign language is more and more important," he says. "Which language is not so important. Any of the global languages are something you could very well use, depending upon where you end up."

Postsecondary Training

Business managers often have a college degree in a subject that pertains to the department they direct or the organization they administer; for example, accounting or economics for a business manager of finance, computer science for a business manager of data processing, engineering or science for a director of research and development. As computer usage grows, many managers are expected to have experience with the information technology that applies to their field.

Graduate and professional degrees are common. Bowe, along with many managers in administrative, marketing, financial, and manufacturing activities, has a master's degree in business administration. Managers in highly technical manufacturing and research activities often have a master's degree or doctorate in a technical or scientific discipline. A law degree is mandatory for business managers of corporate legal departments, and hospital managers generally have a master's degree in health services administration or business administration. In some industries, such as retail trade or the food and beverage industry, competent individuals without a college degree may become business managers.

Other Requirements

There are a number of personal characteristics that help one be a successful business manager, depending upon the specific responsibilities of the position. A manager who oversees other employees should have good communication and interpersonal skills. The ability to delegate work is another important personality trait of a good manager. The ability to think on your feet is often key in business management, according to Bowe. "You have to be able to think extremely quickly and not in a reactionary manner," he says. Bowe also says that a certain degree of organization is important, since managers are often managing several different things simultaneously. Other traits considered important for top executives are intelligence, decisiveness, intuition, creativity, honesty, loyalty, a sense of responsibility, and planning abilities. Finally, the successful manager should be flexible and interested in staying abreast of new developments in his or her industry. "In general, you need to be open to change because your customers change, your market changes, your technology changes," he says. "If you won't try something new, you really have no business being in management."

EXPLORING

To get experience as a manager, start with your own interests. Whether you are involved in drama, sports, school publications, or a part-time job, there are managerial duties associated with any organized activity. These can involve planning, scheduling, managing other workers or volunteers, fund-raising, or budgeting. Local businesses also have job opportunities through which you can get firsthand knowledge and experience of management structure. If you cannot get an actual job, at least try to schedule a meeting with a business manager to talk with him or her about the career. Some schools or community organizations arrange job-shadowing, where you can spend part of a day "shadowing" a selected employee to see what his or her job is like. Joining Junior Achievement is another excellent way to get involved with local businesses and learn about how they work. Finally, take every opportunity to work with computers, since computer skills are vital to today's business world.

EMPLOYERS

There are approximately 7 million general managers and executives employed in the United States. These jobs are found in every industry, and virtually every business in the United States has some form of managerial positions. Obviously, the larger the company is, the more managerial positions it is likely to have. Another factor is the geographical territory covered by the business. It is safe to say that companies doing business in larger geographical territories are likely to have more managerial positions than those with smaller territories.

STARTING OUT

Generally you will need a college degree, although many retail stores, grocery stores, and restaurants hire promising applicants who have only a high school diploma. Job seekers usually apply directly to the manager of such places. Your college placement office is often the best place to start looking for these positions. A number of listings can also be found in newspaper and online help wanted ads.

Many organizations have management trainee programs that college graduates can enter. Such programs are advertised at college career fairs or through college job placement services. Often, however, these management trainee positions in business and government are filled by employees who are already working for the organization and who demonstrate management potential. Jeff Bowe suggests researching the industry you are interested in to find out what might be the best point of entry for that field. "I came into the printing company through customer service, which is a good point of entry because it's one of the easiest things to learn," he says. "Although it requires more technical know-how now than it did then, customer service is still not a bad entry point for this industry."

ADVANCEMENT

Most business management and top executive positions are filled by experienced lower-level managers and executives who display valuable managerial traits, such as leadership, self-confidence, creativity, motivation, decisiveness, and flexibility. In small firms advancement to a higher management position may come slowly, while promotions may occur more quickly in larger firms.

Advancement may be accelerated by participating in different kinds of educational programs available for managers. These are often paid for by the organization. Company training programs broaden knowledge of company policy and operations. Training programs sponsored by industry and trade associations and continuing education courses in colleges and universities can familiarize managers with the latest developments in management techniques. In recent years, large numbers of middle managers were laid off as companies streamlined operations. Competition for jobs is keen, and business managers committed to improving their knowledge of the field and of related disciplines—especially computer information systems—will have the best opportunities for advancement.

Business managers may advance to executive or administrative vice president. Vice presidents may advance to peak corporate positions—president or chief executive officer. Presidents and chief executive officers, upon retirement, may become members of the board of directors of one or more firms. Sometimes business managers establish their own firms.

EARNINGS

Salary levels for business managers vary substantially, depending upon the level of responsibility, length of service, and type, size, and location of the organization. Top-level managers in large firms can earn much more than their counterparts in small firms. Also, salaries in large metropolitan areas, such as New York City, are higher than those in smaller cities. According to the U.S. Department of Labor, all managers had a median yearly income of $70,870 in 2003. To show the range of earnings for general managers, however, the Department notes that those in the computer and information systems had an annual median of $89,740; those in public relations, $64,820; and those at eating and drinking establishments, $37,260.

Again, salaries varied by industry. For example, the median yearly salary for managers in engineering was

$94,470, while those in financial services earned a median of $77,300. A survey by Abbott, Langer, & Associates found that chief executives working for nonprofits had a median yearly salary of $81,000 in 2003. According to the Department of Labor, chief executives officially earned a median of $134,740 annually in 2003. Most executives, however, earn hundreds of thousands—or millions—of dollars more than this annually in benefits and stock options. According to the *New York Times*, the CEO of a major company received $9.2 million in total compensation in 2003.

Benefit and compensation packages for business managers are usually excellent, and may even include such things as bonuses, stock awards, company-paid insurance premiums, use of company cars and aircraft, paid country club memberships, expense accounts, and generous retirement benefits.

WORK ENVIRONMENT

Business managers are provided with comfortable offices near the departments they direct. Top executives may have spacious, lavish offices and may enjoy such privileges as executive dining rooms, company cars, country club memberships, and liberal expense accounts.

Managers often travel between national, regional, and local offices. Top executives may travel to meet with executives in other corporations, both within the United States and abroad. Meetings and conferences sponsored by industries and associations occur regularly and provide invaluable opportunities to meet with peers and keep up with the latest developments. In large corporations, job transfers between the parent company and its local offices or subsidiaries are common.

Business managers often work long hours under intense pressure to meet, for example, production and marketing goals. Jeff Bowe's average workweek consists of 55 to 60 hours at the office. This is not uncommon—in fact, some executive spend up to 80 hours working each week. These long hours limit time available for family and leisure activities.

OUTLOOK

Overall, employment of business managers and executives is expected to grow about as fast as the average through 2012, according to the U.S. Bureau of Labor Statistics. Many job openings will be the result of managers being promoted to better positions, retiring, or leaving their positions to start their own businesses. Even so, the compensation and prestige of these positions make them highly sought after, and competition to fill openings will be intense.

Projected employment growth varies by industry. For example, employment in the service industry, particularly business services, should increase faster than the average, while employment in some manufacturing industries is expected to decline.

The outlook for business managers is closely tied to the overall economy. When the economy is good, businesses expand both in terms of their output and the number of people they employ, which creates a need for more managers. In economic downturns, businesses often lay off employees and cut back on production, which lessens the need for managers.

TO LEARN MORE ABOUT BUSINESS MANAGERS

BOOKS

Greenberg, Keith Elliot. *Bill Bowerman & Phil Knight: Building the Nike Empire.* Woodbridge, Conn.: Blackbirch Press, 1994.

Raatma, Lucia. *Bill Gates: Computer Programmer and Entrepreneur.* Ferguson Career Biographies. New York: Facts On File, 2001.

Ryan, Bernard Jr. *Jeff Bezos: Business Executive and Founder of Amazon.com.* Ferguson Career Biographies. New York: Facts On File, 2005.

Shuker, Nancy. *Elizabeth Arden: Beauty Empire Builder.* Woodbridge, Conn.: Blackbirch Press, 2001.

Wilson, Suzan. *Steve Jobs: Wizard of Apple Computer.* Berkeley Heights, N.J.: Enslow Publishers, 2001.

WEBSITES AND ORGANIZATIONS

For news about management trends, resources on career information and finding a job, and an online job bank, contact

American Management Association
1601 Broadway
New York, NY 10019-7420
Tel: 800-262-9699
http://www.amanet.org

For brochures on careers in management for women, contact

Association for Women in Management
927 15th Street, NW, Suite 1000
Washington, DC 20005
Tel: 202-659-6364
Email: awm@benefits.net
http://www.womens.org

For information about programs for students in kindergarten through high school, and information on local chapters, contact

Junior Achievement

One Education Way

Colorado Springs, CO 80906

Tel: 719-540-8000

Email: newmedia@ja.org

http://www.ja.org

For a brochure on management as a career, contact

National Management Association

2210 Arbor Boulevard

Dayton, OH 45439

Tel: 937-294-0421

Email: nma@nma1.org

http://nma1.org

TO LEARN MORE ABOUT MEG WHITMAN

BOOKS

Cohen, Adam *The Perfect Store: Inside eBay*. Boston: Little Brown, 2002.

Effronn, Marc. *Human Resources in the 21st Century*. New York: John Wiley, 2003.

Heskett, James L. *The Value Profit Chain: Treat Employees Like Customers and Customers Like Employees*. New York: Free Press, 2002.

Stross, Randall E. *eBoys: The First Inside Account of Venture Capitalists at Work*. New York: Ballantine, 2002.

Wachs, Esther. *Why the Best Man for the Job Is a Woman: The Unique Female Qualities of Leadership.* New York: HarperBusiness, 2001.

WEBSITES

"Company Overview: Meg Whitman." ebay.com/ community/aboutebay/overview/management.html. Accessed March 3, 2004.

Fishman, Charles. "Face Time With Meg Whitman." *Fast Company*, May 2001. http://www.fastcompany.com/ magazine/46/facetime.html.

"Meg Whitman." Fortune, http://www.fortune.com/ fortune/powerwomen/snapshot/0,15944,2,00.html.

Fox, Loren. "Meg Whitman." Salon.com, 2003. http:// dir.salon.com/people/bc/2001/11/27/whitman/index. html.

Kerstetter, Jim, "Meg Whitman." Businessweek Online, May 15, 2000. http://www.businessweek.com/2000/ 00_20/b3681011.htm.

Lashinsky, Adam, "100 Fastest Growing Companies: The Meg Machine." Fortune, Sept. 1, 2001. http://www. fortune.com/fortune/fastest/articles/0,15114,473553,00. html.

Lynch, Dianne, "At the Top: Why eBay's Meg Whitman Has Reason to Be Jolly." ABC News, Dec. 5, 2003.

http://www.mrwebauthor.com/eBay/SuccessStory/AtTheTop.html.

McConnell, Ben, "How Meg Whitman and eBay Rule the World." CreatingCustomerEvangelists, 2003. http://www.creatingcustomerevangelists.com/resources/evangelists/meg_whitman.asp.

"Meg Whitman," September 29, 2003. http://www.businessweek.com/magazine/content/03_39/b3851602.htm.

Pepe, Michele, "Meg Whitman." CRN, March 9, 2004. http://www.crn.com/sections/special/top25/top25_02.jhtml?articleId=18822009&_requestid=349159.

Sandsmark, Fred. "Q&A with eBay's Meg Whitman." IQ Magazine, July/August 2001. http://business.cisco.com/prod/tree.taf%3Fasset_id=58046&public_view=true&kbns=1.html.

Stross, Randall, "What an Old Sears Catalog Could Teach eBay Today." *New York Times*, May 9, 2004. http://www.nytimes.com/pages/business/columns/.

"Digital 50: Meg Whitman." Time Digital, http://www.time.com/time/digital/digital50/05.html. Accessed March 3, 2004.

INDEX

Page numbers in *italics* indicate illustrations.

ABOUT THE AUTHOR

Leslie Alan Horvitz is the author of several books about current developments in science, medicine, and politics, as well as scores of magazine articles on business, entertainment, the arts, money laundering, security, and international crime. His most recent books include *Eureka: Scientific Breakthroughs that Changed the World*; *Understanding Depression* (with Dr. Raymond DePaulo), *Wayne: An Abused Child's Story of Courage, Survival and Hope* (with Wayne Theodore), and *Level 4: Virus Hunters of the CDC* (with Joseph McCormick and Susan Fisher-Hoch), as well as the forthcoming *Encyclopedia of War Crimes and Genocide*.